FRED

In memory of R.H.J.

This is a Borzoi Book published by Alfred A. Knopf, Inc.

Copyright © 1987 by Posy Simmonds
All rights reserved under International and Pan-American Copyright Conventions. Published in
the United States by Alfred A. Knopf, Inc., New York. Distributed by Random House, Inc.,
New York. Published in Great Britain by Jonathan Cape Limited, London.
First American Edition   Manufactured in Great Britain
1 3 5 7 9 10 8 6 4 2

Library of Congress Cataloging-in-Publication Data
Simmonds, Posy. Fred.
Summary: The night Sophie and Nick bury their dearly beloved cat, Fred, all Fred's cat
friends arrive to reveal his nighttime self and give him a proper funeral and farewell.
[1. Cats—Fiction.   2. Death—Fiction.   3. Funeral rites and ceremonies—Fiction.
4. Cartoons and comics]   I. Title.   PZ7.S5913Fr 1987 [E] 86-21395
ISBN 0-394-88627-5   ISBN 0-394-98627-X (lib. bdg.)

FRED

POSY SIMMONDS

ALFRED A. KNOPF · NEW YORK

Sophie and Nick sit on the step outside their house feeling sad....

He was quite old

He got very ill...

Yes!

He had **cat flu**

Everyone is sad when they hear the news....

Poor Fred! I am sorry

We'll **miss** him... he used to sleep on our wall...

He used to sleep on my **trash can**

He used to sleep on our **car**!

Fred used to sleep *all* the time.

He also liked eating....

...and purring and sitting on laps...

...but, most of all, he liked sleeping....

...on the ironing board...

...on the washing...

...on top of the fridge.....

....in patches of sunlight....

...and, especially, on beds.

Now Fred is buried at the end of the garden, underneath a bush.....

Nearby are the graves of a guinea pig and a beetle, which Sophie marked with stones....

He was the laziest cat in the world, Fred was...

Fat old Fred

Z at what you're putting on his gravestone?

No, dumbo! You have to write something *nice!*

I dunno what to put....

I'll just write his name...
...*stop* bumping me!

There...

Fred

Soon the children fall asleep...  ...first Nick.... ...and then Sophie...

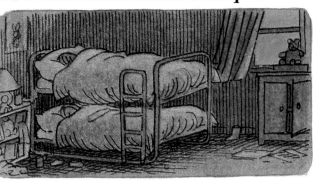

Meeeyow!

Meeow....
...oow..ow...
..Meeow!

!

Nick!
Nicky!

Mnh?

Look! In the garden.... ..a **cat**...

...in a **HAT!**

Can't see!

Can't **SEE!!**

Ssh!

I want to **SEE!!**

Shush!

THERE! Look!

A cat in a hat!

Tsk! They're late!

So late!

Hey! It's **GINGER!** Mrs. Spedding's **Ginger!**

Hey! He's got a digital watch!

He was **OURS!**

YOURS?

YOU...OWNED Fred?!

YES!

YOU...owned the **MOST FAMOUS CAT** in the **WORLD!**

Fred?

Famous?

He wasn't **FAMOUS!** He didn't **DO** anything!

No, he did nuffing!

Did *nuffing*?!

No, he **slept** all the time!

Well, sometimes he took walks ...sometimes he did **wees** on Mrs. Spedding's flowers and she was cross!

Did **WEES?!**

Yes!

HUSH! There are kittens present!

Ah!

Here at Last!

Yes, we're here...

O poor, poor Fred!

Poor Fred is dead!

The most FAMOUS cat in the WORLD!

But WHY was he FAMOUS? .... WHY?

Kindly lower your voice!

But he just SLEPT all day!!

He slept all day... but...at NIGHT..?

At night, Mom put him out...

Yes! And every night, HOW we waited for that moment....

...when the back door would open......

Out you go, Fred... Night, night

...and the lights went out, and all was hushed.....

...and then, Fred would make his bow....

...and start to sing...

MeYOWL!

Fred SANG?!!

.O Caterwauley~wailey~woe...O Woe, O woe weeooo!

Then, one by one, the mourners lay their wreaths and flowers on the grave.

Through the kitchen…down the passage….out of the front door….

Sophie and Nick creep in through the front door....

....tiptoe up the stairs.......and climb into bed.....

...and soon, first Nick....and then Sophie, fall fast asleep.

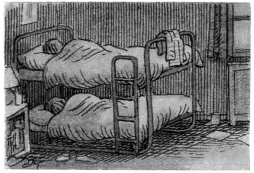  

It's *funny* the next morning.....